SYLVIE ROUHANI

The Blossoming Lotus

AUSTIN MACAULEY PUBLISHERS™
LONDON • CAMBRIDGE • NEW YORK • SHARJAH

A CIP catalogue record for this title is available from the British Library.

ISBN 9781035806423 (Paperback)
ISBN 9781035806430 (ePub e-book)

www.austinmacauley.com

First Published 2023
Austin Macauley Publishers Ltd
1 Canada Square
Canary Wharf
London
E14 5AA

For my daughter, Zoë,
With all my Love,
Mum

POEMS

Lotus:

The Blossoming Lotus is a collection of the poems I wrote over the last 10 years, during which I have experienced heartache, betrayal, hope, joy, poverty, despair, self-loathing, self-love, homelessness, and friendships.

The poems are not in any order: suffering, grieving, healing aren't linear processes. Some days, I feel like a powerful "priestess" – on top of the world, connected to everyone and everything. Other days, I feel like a frightened little girl. However, I am learning to love the frightened child as well as the enlightened Self, including so many other Inner Parts. This, for me, is Healing: caring for, learning from, and loving all aspects of myself.

The message here is that, just like the Lotus Flower growing in muddy water/ life's challenges, we can grow strong and beautiful.

I hope you enjoy reading this collection. My prayer is for my messages to reach those who need them the most.

Sylvie

Lotus

With great determination,
She pushes through the muddy water.
She fixes all her attention on the light
The tiny speck of hope shining above.

Slowly she rises.
She pauses for a moment.
She unfolds her petals.
One at a time.

Finally, she reveals her inner beauty.
Her heart is wide open for all to see.
She shares her wisdom with us:
No matter how murky the water is, it doesn't stop you from blossoming.

I don't know:

I have suffered with depression all my life. "Leave the past in the past," they say. What if the past is still present? Because it is in our body, our mind, and our spirit.

Sometimes I barely have any life-force in me to do all the things I wish to do.

And when things are good, I am always worried something will bring me down. I do the best I can.

I don't know

I choose to live but it doesn't make sense. I don't know how to.

For so many years, I tried to find my purpose in this life, but I've never found it.

The past always haunts me. It robs me of all my energy and joy.

All these demons are lurking in dark corners. They are waiting. The moment I sigh with contentment and happiness; the moment I let my guard down, they jump out at me and drag me into the shadow. My body inert on the cold floor.

Sometimes I just don't want to get up again. I am too tired.

Please, let me lie there in the dust.

Please let me rest.

Support in the present tense:

It's very important to meet people where they are at NOW, even if witnessing their despair is uncomfortable for us.

In truth, we don't know what life has in store for us. Yes, there are things we can control and change but, there are so many different factors at play.

The best we can do is to sit down and to say, "I am here for you, let me know what you need."

Support in the present tense

It doesn't matter how many times someone says, "You will be OK". Right now, you are not OK and if people don't acknowledge your pain and support you where you are at NOW, there might not be a future with you in it.

Rising of the Phoenix

Rise,
Rise from your ashes.
Yes, there is nothing left but you.
You in your magnificence.
You in your glory.
Listen to yourself:
"I can lose everything and everyone, but it is fine: I've me!"
"I stand tall and strong in the middle of my life's rubbles."
Your world as you knew it is gone.
Destroyed.
Wrecked.
Rise my child,
Rise and rebuild.
You can do it.
They can destroy it a bit more if that is what they want to do.
Let them take your things too.
That is all they are: things!
They can't destroy you.
You: your heart and soul.
God knows they tried but they can't take them from you
Rise
Dance
Stomp

Cry

Scream

Laugh

Live

Be

Feel

Yes, you can do it.

*

Rising of the Phoenix:

The Phoenix rises from her ashes, triumphantly spreading her wings. She's been through so much: homelessness, heartbreak, betrayal, a nervous breakdown. Her entire world was destroyed. Here she is now, reborn, and ready to fly.

*

In the space of a year, I went through a traumatic breakup, my daughter moved in with her father. I later became homeless and was placed within an abusive care setting.

This poem describes the desire to survive and to move forward while also experiencing intense emotional pain.

Waiting:

For so long, I was waiting for those who hurt and abandoned me to come back and love me – as a child and then as a woman.

Attachment Trauma is real and painful. It destroys lives. This changed for me when I stopped thinking I was crazy and broken; when I accepted this is what I've done to survive, and I was suffering deeply. It was better to wait for the adult around me to change than to face reality and die. No child can live without love. No one can live without love.

People suffering with Attachment Trauma aren't "Love Addicts": they are experiencing emotional flashbacks which trigger old patterns created in childhood to survive being hurt, neglected, and rejected.

Waiting

I am waiting.
I've been waiting for years now
For Mum and Dad to love and protect me.
For those who destroyed my world to come back and rebuild it.
For those who left me behind in pain to come back and soothe it.
For those who slapped and hurt me to come back and kiss it all better.
For those who said they loved me and then abandoned me, to come back and love me for real.
For you to pick up the phone you never answer.
For you to open the door you never really opened in the first place.
For you to show me what true love is as you promised before you broke my heart.
For you to be by my side when you ran away so fast and so long ago.
I was a little girl waiting for love. I am a woman waiting for love
I can't wait for the day I will stop waiting. I can't wait for the day I will start living.
I just don't know how to stop doing one thing and how to start doing another...
So, for now, I do the only thing I know:
I am waiting for those who are gone
I am waiting for those who are never coming back.

Birth:

Spring is upon us. Flowers are piercing through Mother Earth. It's a new beginning. There is so much we can learn from Mother Nature about the process of birth, the natural process of change and adaptation. Things happen at the right timing, and it takes patience as well as trust.

Birth

I came out of Mother Gaia's womb,
Looking at Father Sun, up above,
Its bright light blinding me.
I felt the fresh air on my face.
The earth was pulsing all around me,
Pushing me up towards the sky.
I smelled the grass and the trees,
Heard singing birds and buzzing bees.
I felt the cold water coursing through me,
Nourishing me.
I am growing,
Blossoming.
Living.

Thank you:

I wrote this poem when I had one of those difficult days, and it took all my strength to get up, to eat, to bathe and more. When I allow myself to rest, I am sometimes filled with guilt. Depression robs us of our energy and of our joy; any small step we take is a huge one. Yes, resting is also acting for our well-being.

Thank you

for opening your eyes.
Thank you
for making that cup of coffee.
Thank you
for going back to bed.
Thank you
for making that sandwich.
Thank you
for running that bath.
Thank you
for letting me rest.
Thank you
for not forcing me to go out into the world.
Thank you
for letting me be with the pain.
Thank you
for not judging me.
Thank you
for loving me just as I am.
Thank you
for being strong enough to go through all of this.
Thank you
for being my best friend:
You are all I have.

Toxic positivity:

Of course, feeling positive is great but when it is used to minimise our pain and completely ignore our difficulties, it isn't healthy. It is more heartbreaking when we do it to ourselves or when those statements come from the people we open our heart to. It gives us the message that we are pessimistic, and that we aren't trying hard enough. We need to be allowed to share our despair and suffering, no matter how difficult it might be to hear it, so we can heal in total acceptance.

Toxic positivity

"Keep your chin up."

"Stay positive."

"Everything will be all right."

But I feel

Scared,

Lonely,

Stressed.

Somehow, I keep going, slowly, step by step. I act. I rest. I take a bit more action. I rest some more. I shake. I cry. I scream. I sit down and listen to the voice within. I am going back to the Source. I am going back to my centre.

I go back to myself before I lose myself in the chaos of my life.

It isn't about me keeping my chin up or staying positive and denying my truth.

It is about lovingly holding myself through the sadness, the hopelessness, and the fears.

Whole:

A moment of feeling at one with the Universe and everything/ everybody in It.

When I walk in nature, I am always amazed by the fact that, on a cellular level, we are all the same as the Sun, the Moon, the sky, animals, even vegetation, as well as space and all the planets in it.

We are all made of the same stuff!

Whole

I am the Sun
I am the Moon
I am the Air
I am the Earth
I am Fire
I am Water
I go places
I stand tall and still
I am warm
I am cold
I am everywhere
Above and below
North, South, West and East
I embrace all
I am God
I am Goddess
I am the Universe

Rainbows everywhere:

Rainbows: colours of the Chakras, of the Universe – Life itself.

Colours of the LGBTQA+ community. I am Bi. I came out in my late 30s. It took me a long time to get to know myself.

We are all made of light.

We are all made of rainbows.

Rainbows everywhere

Red

Orange

Yellow

Green

Pink

Blue

Indigo

Light

The colours of the rainbow.
The colours of my pastels.
The colours on my fingertips.
The colours of my soul.
The Colours of the Universe.

Red for grounding
Orange for pleasure
Yellow for inner power.
Green for healing
Pink for unconditional love
Blue for communication
Indigo for intuition
Light for connection.
Colours within me, all around me.
Rainbows everywhere.

Morning prayer:

I no longer pray for or set the intention to have a "good" day or a "positive" day. I pray that, no matter what kind of day is ahead of me, I can love and support me through it all,

Feelings of sadness, of anger and of discomfort don't mean we failed in some way or that we are less than.

Morning prayer

I no longer ask the Universe for a good day.
I now ask that, no matter what happens today, I can love and care for myself through it all.

Eternity:

This poem describes a moment of pure joy. Moment of inner peace, between inner storms. It is a reminder that, in truth, we are one. In truth, we are all made of the same stuff. In truth, we are eternal, maybe not in a human form, but I like to think that, when we die, all our "particles" just go back everywhere in the Universe.

Eternity

I am from the universe,
One of many stars,
Shining bright and eternal.
I am from Mother Earth,
I came out of her womb dancing with joy,
Excited about this new life.
I am one with you,
Sad, happy, vulnerable, strong...Eternal
You are my family:
My brothers, my sisters, my mothers, my fathers...
And I love you, I love me, I love us.
There are more than pain and sadness in me:
There are Joy and Love.
There is you and there is me...
Lifetimes after lifetimes,
For Eternity.

No:

It needs to stop, this obsession of telling survivors of incest/child sexual abuse who have been through horrible things, to learn an important life lesson: that, somehow, we chose this for some karmic reasons! We are not martyrs, we were victims. We were children.

None of this is helpful, nor is it compassionate.

No

No, I didn't choose this.

It wasn't a gift.

It wasn't a blessing.

It wasn't a lesson to learn.

It didn't happen for me.

I was a child.

It was rape.

What happened, happened:

I used to worry about the past and how I could have done better! I used to question my every move.

I would also be petrified about the future: what is going to happen to me? I only foresaw darkness. I still do, sometimes. I'm learning to trust myself and the Universe. It's an ongoing process. When I'm scared, I hold myself with self-compassion.

What happened, happened

I can't undo the past.
I no longer want to know "why".

What happened, happened.

I can only live here and now.
I no longer wish to give a meaning to it all.

What will happen, will happen.

I can't control the future either.
I now decide to embrace the unknown and the chaos.
I now decide to see my life as a great adventure.

How am I still here?

There have been times when I was so surprised to be alive! Sometimes I wished I wasn't. I used to curse the day I opened Pandora's box of my past of child abuse – physical, sexual, and emotional abuse and neglect. Sometimes, during my journey, I felt that if the abuse didn't kill me, my recovery would.

Some individuals don't know how painful it is to remember and to FEEL what we have, for so long, tried to forget, to survive, and not to feel the terror of the past, all over again.

Today, I'm glad I'm here. I am no longer surprised: I am a tough cookie!

How am I still here?

How am I still here?
I asked myself this question so many times.
I screamed till I lost my voice.
I cried till I was dry.
I hurt so much, I wanted to rip my heart out.
I curled up in a ball till I disappeared.
I was so numb, I felt dead.
I wished I was dead.
How am I still here?
I am because my heart doesn't want to stop beating even when I want it to stop.
I am because, somewhere within me, there is this ever-shining light.

A&E for a broken heart:

Seven years ago, as well as going through a traumatic breakup, I was homeless. I was placed in a care setting for a year. Some of my friends didn't understand: "But you have somewhere to go." Yes, I had a roof over my head; however, I had lost MY home, my safe place. I was also bullied by the woman who was supposed to care for me. I had lost so much in such a short period of time. I felt so alone. I was so scared. I was grieving. My heart was broken.

A&E for a broken heart

Yes, they found me four walls and a roof.
Yes, I will have shelter, food, and warmth this winter.
One question, though: Is there such a place as an A&E for broken hearts?
I am holding mine in my cupped hands.
Look how broken it is.
Look at it!
So, please tell me what to do.
Tell me what to do.
Because I don't know anymore.

Goodbye:

Breakups are one of the most painful experiences in life. Saying goodbye is the hardest thing of all. We do go through the five stages of grief after the loss of a relationship. 1) Denial, 2) Anger, 3) Bargaining, 4) Depression, 5) Acceptance. (People say they are, in fact, seven stages, others push it to 12 stages! 5 is enough!)
It is safe to say that when we can finally say "Goodbye", we have reached a place of acceptance. It takes time to get there, but we eventually do.

Goodbye

I will not send you this letter I kept in my bag for so long.
I will no longer knock at your door.
I will no longer walk up and down your street.
There is only one word left to say:
Goodbye.

It is so very sad:

Each year, Mother's Day is a bitter-sweet celebration: I do not have a mother to celebrate. For my own safety and safety, as well as my daughter's, I went "No Contact" with her, years ago.

Many told me: "But she is your mother, she too suffered, and she did the best she could."

Not all mothers are loving and caring: they hurt so much, they hurt themselves and those around them. It is helpful, to a degree, to understand our mothers 'past, but it is not our job to care for them, nor is it our responsibility to repair our relationship if they are not interested in facing the damage they created.

It is possible to feel compassion, but it doesn't mean opening your heart and arms back to her. Do what you feel is best for your happiness.

It is so very sad

You are strong.
You are courageous too.
To survive what you have survived proves it.
It is so sad that you have lost your heart and soul in your battle for survival.
It is so sad that you had to justify and normalise what they did to you.
It is so sad that you had to justify and normalise what you did to us.
It is so sad that you never had the chance
To love and to be loved,
To trust and to be trusted,
To be happy in your own heart,
To be a mother to your children.
It is so sad I must protect myself from you.
Sad, indeed, that I must leave you behind to be happy and safe.
This is how abuse wrecks families.

Temple:

This poem describes a moment of inner peace, feeling safe within my body.

I was born with a congenital myopathy – muscle wasting disease – I was late walking and, when I finally did, I was wobbly on my legs, and experienced pain, and fatigue. I cannot run or swim, nor can I lift heavy things or stand up or walk for too long.

Teased in school for being skinny and weak, I grew up hating my body. Now I am more accepting and loving of my body.

I am grateful I can walk, move and breathe (some people, with more severe muscular dystrophies, can't even breathe unaided), and exercises are overrated!

Temple

You are my temple.
You are my home.
You are my sanctuary.
I am safe.
I am protected.
I am supported.
I am loved.
When I go within, I find there all the Love and the Light of the Universe.
All that I ever need is within me, I am content.

Opening:

I drafted this poem while I was exploring the Inner Goddess, the spiritual aspect of sex, the Yoni (Sanskrit name of the vagina) with its cycles and its link to the Moon's phases.

As a victim and a survivor of child sexual abuse, I have a desire to reframe sex and what it means for me, but, to be honest, this is a part of my journey that is difficult to explore. This can't be rushed.

I highly recommend the book *Vagina* by Naomi Wolf.

Opening

Yoni

Womb

Home

Sanctuary

Void

Beginning of all life

Beginning of all creations

Centre of all energies

Warmth

Security

Safety

Grounding

Goddess Within

Blank pages of my life:

So many questions and no answers. Not knowing what will happen tomorrow/ in the future is so scary, especially if we grew up with unpredictable characters.

Since I wrote this poem, I'm learning to focus on one day at a time and that, no matter what happens, I'll treat myself with self-compassion and tender loving care. Some days are easier than others!

Blank pages of my life

I am petrified to face the unknown without a name. If my life was a book, it would be like turning the page to the next chapter only to find the rest of this book completely blank. Where is the rest of the story? What is going to happen? Why are the pages empty? What happened to the writer? How is the story going to unfold? What happened to my life? So many questions. No answers to be found.

Closed door:

As a result of the abandonment and the emotional neglect, I suffered as a child/ teenager, I used to hold on to unavailable people, waiting for them to open their heart/ door to me.

For so long, I was starving for love and attention, and one of my Inner Children was ready to do or say anything not to be alone, not to lose her partner. I was also ashamed of this part of me, until I felt her despair and understood that, if she didn't hold on to the adults around her, denying how horrible they were, she would have died. I wouldn't be here, alive and kicking.

I highly recommend the books *Self-Compassion* and *Fierce Self-Compassion* by Dr Kristin Neff, PhD.

Check out her website at www.selfcompassion.org

Closed door

Knock, knock, knock
Anybody there?
I have so much love to give you.
Please open the door.
Please love me too.

Inner child:

There is a lot written on "healing and loving the inner child." In fact, we have many inner parts that need our love and compassion. The concepts of IFS (Internal Family System) changed the way I treat myself and all my inner parts that have suffered so much.

Dr Richard Schwartz, PhD, authored a wonderful book: *No Bad Parts*. I highly recommend it.

Inner child

Cry, my child,
I cry with you.
Hurt, my child,
I hurt with you.
Scream out your pain, my child,
I scream with you.
Love my child,
I love with you.
I love you.

Sanctuary:

This poem describes the aftermath of a very painful breakup. When you love someone very much, they become your sanctuary. Mine had just been destroyed, and it was disorienting, messy and scary.

Sanctuary

You were my home.
You were warm.
I felt safe there.
Then this tornado ripped you apart.
I woke up from my dream:
All the walls were gone!
I felt suddenly so cold. Vulnerable.
I looked around me:
What a mess!
I had no choice but to gather my things.
I stood up and started walking.
I couldn't stop looking backwards in shock.
I kept falling on the debris of what was my sanctuary: you.
I fell so many times.
I hurt myself again, and again.
You were my home.
You were so warm.
Somehow, I kept going forward.
Today, I am still on that path
I'm still looking behind me from time to time,
And my feet slip now and again.
It doesn't hurt so much now.
I think I will be OK.
You were once my home.
Today, you are my home no more...

Healing anger:

I was told not to be angry by many, myself included. Anger is seen as bad and destructive. It certainly was in the home where I grew up. I tried to be good, but I, too, was deeply hurting myself by swallowing down my emotions.

Once I understood that I could use my anger as a creative energy to make changes, to set boundaries, to say "no," I no longer felt ashamed of it.

Anger is a natural response to being hurt by those who abuse us. It is an inner part of us saying: "They had no right to treat me this way!" or, in the face of injustice: "This isn't right nor fair! What can I do to rectify this?"

Healing anger

They say: "Do not hold on to anger."
My anger is what drives me to forge on.
It expresses my passion to build a better life,
To fight for justice,
To stand up for myself, for my values, for my needs,
To set up boundaries, to protect myself.
There is nothing wrong with anger!!
So, don't tell me not to be angry.
It is my right to be angry.
And I will shout as loud as I want to.
I don't care.

Brave little soldier:

There is a lot of pressure to heal, to do the work. "You work, and you work on your recovery." We are told to set goals and to act.

We are told not to be a "victim", but to show our strength and our survivor's skills.

We were victims. We are survivors too. Both parts are within us. Both need to be validated and loved.

Resting is also important. Resting is still taking care of ourselves. Resting is another act of recovery.

Brave little soldier

I am thinking of you,
Brave little soldier.
You have been resting for quite awhile
And now you are gently coming back to us.
Hello, brave little soldier!
It is so nice to see you again.
I admire you:
It takes real courage to face this world and to say
"You know what, I need to rest, I need to look after myself."
Even the most courageous soldiers, like us
need to know when to leave the battle,
To lead a happy life.

Loving so much, losing so much:

The breakup felt so sudden. One day my entire life was centred around this one person. The next, this person was gone, creating an emptiness, a void that terrified me and the sudden silence deafening.

This was a flashback of the emptiness I felt as a child. It hurt so much.

Loving so much, losing so much

How can we love so much?
And then lose so much?
Where did it all go?
One day we are so close.
One day we are apart.
How can we love so much?
And then lose so much?
It's all so quiet.
One day we talk and talk.
One day, deafening silence.
How can we love so much?
And then lose so much?
I really don't know...
More silence,
More nothing.

Accepting the pain:

After years of trying to avoid my pain, as I was advised to, I read *Self-Compassion* by Dr Kristin Neff, PhD. I've learned to love myself when I was suffering. I've learned to treat myself with tender loving care. Of course, some days are easier than others, it's a process, but, for me, it changed a lot of things, within my heart and soul.

We can talk about our pain. We can dissect it. We try and reframe it, but, if we don't FEEL it, it can't shift.

Accepting the pain

I meditated my pain away.
It didn't work.
I prayed my pain away,
It didn't work.
I reframed and intellectualised my pain away,
It didn't work.
I drank and smoked my pain away,
It didn't work.
I tried to leave it all behind.
I tried to not think about it.
I tried to "look on the bright side".
Nothing worked.
There was one thing left to do:
Accepting its existence.

Human:

Experiencing gratitude for all the good things in our lives is great. It isn't so great when gratitude is imposed on others or sold as a magic tool in recovery.

We can feel gratitude and still acknowledge what is difficult. Sometimes, our pain is so great we can't feel gratitude for anything. It doesn't make us "bad", it makes us human, a being who needs love and support.

Human

Sharing my difficulties doesn't make me ungrateful.
Sharing my pain and sorrows doesn't make me negative.
It makes me human.
Have some compassion.

New ways:

Playing with words, describing a change of perspective. I still hurt, this is an inevitable part of life, but now, I FEEL it, I embrace it with love and compassion.

New ways

Hurting
Denying
Hiding
Escaping
Lying
I am done with it all!
Still hurting
Accepting
Revealing
Standing
Healing
New ways of dealing with it all

I am not OK:

"Fake it until you can make it!" is a popular saying in recovery. But is it always wise to advise "faking it"?

For me, it is a "No, thank you": I've already had to fake I was never abused, that I was happy and thriving. Healing isn't faking it; it is lovingly embracing any inner obstacles/schemas stopping us from living a full life. Self-compassion, kindness and acceptance are key.

Personally, I no longer want to pretend!

I am not OK

I don't want to hide in another relationship and pretend I am OK.
I don't want to put a smile on my face and act and pretend I am OK.
I don't want to open my door and let you in and pretend I am OK.
I don't want to open my mouth, speak empty words, and pretend I am OK.
I don't want to get out in this scary world and pretend I am OK.
I no longer want to pretend so you can all be happy.

I know:

I wrote this poem for my daughter. She was having a difficult time and I could really relate to her feelings. I just wanted her to know that I understood her, that I am here, for her every step of the way, on her journey through life's ups and downs.

I know

I know you can give your heart to someone for them to carelessly break it.
I know they say you don't try enough while not giving you the support you need.
I know they encourage you to speak up and, when you do, they shut you up.
I know they blame you for what others did to you.
I know, Darling, I know.

Morning:

A joyful and light-hearted poem, celebrating the first morning of spring after a long dark winter. It is always such a joy to wake up to birds singing in the garden.

The sun, the flowers, the breeze, all lift my spirit. They bring our best smiles and happiness all around.

Morning

Quiet morning.
I am half asleep.
I am half awake.
Looking forward to this new day.
I stay still with my breathing
In, out, in, out.
Calm
Peaceful
Content
Outside, birds are joyfully singing
"Good morning!!"
"Good morning!!"

Universal truth:

A lot is happening in the world, here in the UK, all the way to Ukraine…

It is normal and understandable to feel anxiety and fear. It is a time to take loving care of ourselves, first, and of each other.

When the world's chaos overwhelms me, I find hope in the Buddhist guidance that says peace in the world starts within me and within my little corner of the world, with my loved ones and my community.

Universal truth

The world isn't safe right now.
It scares me.
I feel hopeless.
So, I remind myself:
Love and Harmony in the World starts with
Love and Harmony within me,
And then, they can extend
To my loved ones.
To my community
To my country,
To the World
To the Universe.
In truth, we are One.

Inner liberation:

Yes, some put us in a cage. I grew up in one. It was suffocating. It took me years to find that key! It took me years to get out of it. I didn't know I had options. I didn't know I could leave if I was mistreated. I didn't know I could say "No".

What a liberation it was to find that key!!

Inner liberation

For so long, I was held in a cage.
My life, behind bars, just a mirage.
All this time waiting for someone to liberate me,
For so long, not knowing I had the key.

Welcome home, my dear:

I experienced homelessness twice. Both at the end of unhealthy relationships. The first time, I ended up in a women's refuge. It wasn't a pleasant place. The second time was because of a "last minute, before I move in" breakup then I was placed in a care setting for single, homeless individuals with mental illnesses. It was horrible.

Losing your home is deeply traumatising, even if you have a "roof" over your head. Life can change in a minute for the worse. Let's be compassionate to those whose life fell apart.

Welcome home, my dear

Close the door behind you, my dear.
You don't have to deal with the world anymore.
You can relax now, my dear:
Kick your shoes off
And put the kettle on.
Grab a blanket, my dear:
You don't have to feel the cold anymore.
Take a deep breath, let the tension go, my dear:
This is your space; you are safe here.
Rejoice, my dear:
After losing a roof,
You have finally found a Home.

Offering to the sun:

This poem describes a beautiful experience during meditation. I suffer a lot in winter, as I hate being cold. In spring and in summer, my mood improves, I flourish with all the flowers, trees, and Mother Nature.

To be a witness to it all, and to feel a part of it, is amazing. I learn to let go. I let Nature support me. There is still some resistance from an Inner Part of me who feels she can't fully let go: She needs to stay on alert to protect herself. I listen to her and invite to join in the experience, even just for a few minutes.

Offering to the sun

I must have been a sunflower in a past life:
As soon as the sun is out,
I turn my head towards Him.
I close my eyes and feel
His warmth,
His light,
His energy.
I open myself wide to it all.
I gladly offer myself to Him.
And I am all light,
Luminous,
Glorious,
At one with everything.

The games we play:

After a breakup, it can be quite hard to let go, to accept it is over. For those of us suffering from Attachment Trauma, we will find any excuses to see this person again: we need closure, we need to check if it is over. We want one last night of passion or, at least, a kiss. We look at their social media, turning into stalkers. We are in pain and will do anything to not feel it. Until, hopefully, we reach a point of complete acceptance. Hopefully, at this stage, we aren't half dead after trying everything to rebuild a relationship that was never real to begin with.

The games we play

Have I lost you again?
Is it how it's going to be now:
Hide and seek?
Peek-a-boo?
One step forward,
Three steps back?
I've done it before:
It's just like twisting that knife deeper in the wounds.
Nothing good can come out of that.
I'd rather have you forever
Or lose you forever.
I am tired of the games we play.

New beginning:

Joyful beginnings can still bring up a lot of confusion and pain for survivors of child abuse and neglect. It might sound strange, but it makes sense: some of us grew up in chaotic households in which moments of happiness were rare, flitting, not to be trusted. When we tried something new, we might have been told we would fail. So, some of us stopped trying.

Growing up and trying to build our own life, starting anything new, taking that first leap of faith can bring terror up.

We can look around us and follow the example of the young bird, feeling the fear but taking that jump anyway. Otherwise, how is it ever going to fly?

New beginning

A new beginning,
A new life.
A young bird is jumping out of her nest,
Flying high,
Flying free,
In the blue sky,
Into eternity.
I would have never imagined feeling
So light,
So happy,
Getting so close to the sun so bright
Flapping my wings so joyfully!

One person:

Meeting a young Inner Part who has been waiting, waiting, waiting, for Love. There is nothing else she wants more, so she waited, anxiously, for someone to come to the door.

Years later, I was able to recognise her existence within me. I was able to listen to her, to really hear her, and, most importantly, to bear witness to her suffering and to create a safe space for her, in my heart.

I no longer tried to fix her, to make her change the way she was feeling, or shaming her for needing/ wanting so much love. She started to feel calmer. Glad I was there to guide her.

One person

I saw this little girl in me this morning.
She was sitting in front of a door for a while,
Waiting for it to open, waiting for Love.
But, this morning, the door was ajar.
She stood up and pushed it.
A bright light welcomed her.
Bright light full of Hope and full of Love.
There was a beautiful person waiting for her.
It was me; I was waiting for her.
I took her in my arms and kissed her.
"I am so happy you are here now.
You don't have to be alone anymore."
This morning, we merged into one person.

Self-compassion:

Dr Kristin Neff, PhD, pioneered, with Chris Germer, Mindful Self-Compassion, which comprises three elements:

1. Mindfulness: If we aren't in our body, we can't feel our emotions stored in it. We won't notice when we are stressed, low or angry. We can't soothe ourselves through our experiences. Mindfulness is the way to sit with and allow our emotions, as they are, without any judgement. For instance: "This is hard." Or: "I am feeling so sad, right now."

2. Humanity: When we are suffering, it is natural to feel alone. We can, gently, remind ourselves that, in fact, suffering is part of being human. This isn't to minimise our pain but to remind us we aren't alone. For instance: "Many parents are going through a similar situation with their teens."

3. Kindness: It is offering some reassuring and loving words when we are living through a challenging time. "I am going to take loving care of myself today." Or "You are doing your very best right now, it is OK for me to rest."

For more information, go on: www.selfcompassion.org

Self-compassion

When you are having a difficult day,
What do you tell yourself?
"Why can't I be happy?"
"What is wrong with me?"
"I am such a failure."
When a friend is having a difficult time,
What do you tell her?
"I am sorry, this is such a difficult time for you."
"You are doing your best."
"You are amazing."
What is self-compassion?
It is talking to yourself as you would a dear friend.
A friend who is sad and needs,
Love, Compassion, and kindness.
Dear friend, you need your own
love,
compassion,
and kindness.

Teamwork:

So much information out there, from: "You are the master of your own life. Only you can create your own reality." To: "It is the will of God/ Higher Power, not yours."

The truth is some people need to "let and let God/ Higher Power", they need to trust their journey, God/The Universe, and, ultimately, themselves.

Others might need to take more actions to help the process of creating a life that most resonates with them.

The thing is, it's teamwork: pray or chant or meditate (to God, a Higher Power, the Universe...), receive guidance and act on the guidance. When we find our own rhythm through this, your inner world is slowly shifting to one filled with love, acceptance, and compassion through everything that happens around us.

Teamwork

It isn't us having total control over our destiny.
It isn't the Universe having total control over our destiny, either:

It is teamwork.
It is us, at one, with the Universe.

It is us awakened to our true nature:
We are the Universe!

No demon, just human:

Natural responses to childhood trauma are often demonised, pathologised, which adds shame to the already exciting feeling of loathing some of us might experience. Sadly, survivors and victims of child abuse hear those words of "wisdom" from places where they hope to find support and love, places of faith and worship.

As if those moments of inner turmoil aren't scary enough, they are called "Inner Darkness", "Demons", and the people experiencing them are labelled "mad", "possessed", "dysfunctional".

We are all humans hurting, to some degree. Let's support each other.

No demon, just human

Those aren't demons to fight against.
This isn't a fundamental darkness we need to vanquish
This is no "ego" to tame.
Those aren't signs of madness.
Those are human emotions.
Those are natural responses to being deeply hurt.
Those are parts of us needing our love, our acceptance and our
Compassion.

Little caterpillar:

Healing, recovering, changing from the inside out aren't magical moments: they are painful. "It gets harder before it gets better." This isn't always the case! For some of us, the healing process is as difficult as the abuse (and the neglect) we've endured.

What enhances this pain is the judgement others have about it: "You aren't trying hard enough." Or they come up with lists of things to try... So, we believe them, we try harder, or we tick things off the list, desperate not to feel anything that isn't joy.

These heartbreaking moments are natural, but they are also tiring, in mind, body and spirit. Those are times for feeling, for resting, for nurturing; not for doing, not for fixing.

It is tough to transform into a beautiful butterfly! These caterpillars need love, kindness, and compassion.

Little caterpillar

I've wrapped myself up in so many layers.
One by one, these are falling off,
The pain is so overwhelming.
I'm losing parts of myself I no longer need.
Nevertheless, I need to shade those layers off.
There are so many of them.
This transformation feels never-ending.
Agonising.
I just want to disappear.
I am a caterpillar trapped in her cocoon:
Will I ever escape it and fly?

A smile:

A light-hearted, joyful poem written when I was back from a walk at my local park: I was smiling, and people smiled back at me. Some people smiled at me, and I returned the smile with joy.

It was beautiful and gave me hope that there is still some kindness in the world amidst the recent events.

If it feels right, smile, and pass the joy around.

A smile

A smile is
Contagious,
Infectious,
Glorious.
It's a merry-go-round.
Please, pass it around,
Because joy has no bound.

Letter to my younger self:

Here is a letter/poem I wrote for a small inner child of mine.

Therapies such as Gestalt Therapy and Internal Family System enable us to meet, connect and listen to our Inner Parts. It is powerful, moving and cathartic.

During Gestalt therapy, last year, I met so many helpless, sad, angry, and vulnerable parts of me who needed to feel loved, heard, and safe.

It is a good exercise to write letters to your inner Parts, but they are many other ways to communicate with them, too (for those who don't like to write!)

Letter to my younger self

Dear Child

I am so sorry you are in so much pain. You have been for so long.
I am sorry the people you loved the most, hurt you the most.
They couldn't love you, they just couldn't.
I am sorry you lost your home, and you don't feel safe where you are. You feel so disorientated. Lost.
I wish I could tell you when the pain will stop and if things will ever get better.
I wish I had a magic wand to make it all better.
I wish I could kiss the pain and the tears away.
I am here for you, I really am.
I am listening to you.
You are loved.
You are safe.
Let's hold hands and let's never let go.

Love & Light,

Sylvie

Resources

Websites:

- **Co-dependent Anonymous (CODA)** www.coda-uk.org/
- **Beating Trauma – Elizabeth Corey** www.BeatingTrauma.com/
- **Emerging From Broken – Darlene Ouimet** htts//www.emergingfrombroken.com/
- **Baggage Reclaim – Natalie Lue** (Everything on how to get out of the vicious cycle of unhealthy relationships) https://www.baggagereclaim.co.uk/
- **Pandora's Project** (Lots of resources about all types of sexual abuse and there is a forum too) https://pandys.org/intro.html
- **Elefriends** (Online Support Forum for those suffering from mental health difficulties and needing to reach out – Mind) https://www.elefriends.org.uk/
- **Survivors UK** (for male survivors) https://www.survivorsuk.org/about-us
- **For Male Survivors of Rape & Sexual Abuse | Pandora's Project** https://pandys.org/malesurvivors.html

Books:

- **The Courage to Heal** by Ellen Bass & Laura Davis
- **The Courage to Heal Workbook** by Laura Davis
- **Co-dependent No More** and **Beyond Co-dependency** by Melody Beattie
- **Addiction To Love** and **The Art of Changing** by Susan Peabody
- **Mr Unavailable & the Fallback Girl** and **The Dreamer and the Fantasy Relationship** by Natalie Lue
- **The Sexual Healing Journey: A guide for Survivors of Sexual Abuse** by Wendy Maltz
- **Vagina: A New Biography** by Naomi Wolf
- **Self-Compassion** by Dr Kristin Neff, PhD
- **No Bad Parts** by Dr Richard Schwartz, PhD
- **The Body Keeps the Score: Brain, Mind, and the Body in the Healing of Trauma** by Bessel van der Kolk
- **In the Realm of The Hungry Ghosts: Close Encounters with Addiction** by Gabor Mate

(All these books are available at amazon.co.uk – paperback and Kindle)

Therapy/ Coaching and other services, in the UK and online

- **One In Four**: counselling Services by survivors of CSA, for survivors of CSA. http://www.oneinfour.org.uk/
- **Mosac** Supporting non abusing parents and carers of sexually abused children http://www.mosac.org.uk/
- **NAPAC** Offers support for adults survivors and training for who support them. https://napac.org.uk/
- **Cassel Centre** offers affordable counselling in South East London http://www.casselcentre.org.uk/
- **The Survivors Trust** – offers support and guidance http://thesurvivorstrust.org/find-support/london-england/
- **Haven** Charity Providing Counselling Support to Victims of Domestic & Sexual Abuse Across London... http://www.havennetwork.org.uk/
- **Into The Light** (London) Offers counselling, information, support and resources for people who have experienced child sexual abuse and those that support them: http://www.intothelight.org.uk/about/
- **Assunta Cucca** – Coaching & Employee: engagement: www.kokoroconsultancy.co.uk
- **Karen Isbister** – Becoming Whole. I highly recommend her therapy services. She offers: Abuse counselling; PTSD therapy; C-PTSD therapy; Depression and anxiety treatment and more! – All available in person or online, she lives in Australia. She offers concession fees when places available. – www.becomingwhole.co.au

SYLVIE ROUHANI

Lives in South East London with her daughter and her cat. She is a passionate child abuse and mental health activist. She writes a blog – 'Winter Turns into Spring' – and poetry – *The Blossoming Lotus* – to raise awareness about these important topics.

She is a guest blogger for The C-PTSD Foundation.

Ingram Content Group UK Ltd.
Milton Keynes UK
UKHW020124230623
423866UK00004B/22

9 781035 806423